Washday Pockets

Also by Sharon Kernot and published by Ginninderra Press
In the Shadows of the Garden

Sharon Kernot

Washday Pockets

Acknowledgements

Special thanks to Martin Johnson, Helen Lindstrom,
Gary MacRae, Ken Vincent and Cathy Young for their constant
support and encouragement during the writing of this collection.

Some of these poems have appeared in
Common Ground
Beyond the Shimmering
Rewired: Friendly Street Poets 32
Catch Fire: Friendly Street Poets 33
After the Race: Friendly Street Poets 34
Gawler Poetry Reader #1, #2 and #3
The Mozzie
NEW Voices: Selected Poems from North Eastern Writers
Parenting Express
Permanent Waves
Re-Placement: AAWP anthology
Social Alternatives
The Studio Journal
Tamba
Valley Micropress (New Zealand)
The Write Angle

Washday Pockets
ISBN 978 1 74027 644 3
Copyright © text Sharon Kernot 2010
Cover: Gary MacRae

First published 2010
Reprinted 2015

GINNINDERRA PRESS
PO Box 3461 Port Adelaide SA 5015
www.ginninderrapress.com.au

Contents

Voices	9
Making Tea	10
Millipedes	11
The Shed	12
the hole	14
Slowly	16
poetry workshop	18
Empty Rooms	20
In the bathroom	21
Blood Work	22
Tartan	24
Lilies	25
Superstition	26
Sex Scene	28
Mrs Brown	30
Alien	31
At Twelve	33
Thirteen	34
Sewing (the artist's wife)	36
Gone!	37
Teenage Retreat	38
Insomnia	39
Still Living	41
A Starlit Sky	42
Washday Pockets	43
Walking	44
Ironing Sheets	45
Burnt	46
Suburban Villanelle	47
Weeds	48

Let's Play	49
She-Mail	51
Without Punctuation Marks	52
Insomniac dreams	53
Driving Lessons	54
Mother & Child	56
The Old Lifts	57
Bricks	60
Father and Son	61
Winter	62
Breath	63
Cooking	65
Beneath a blue moon	67
With Green Stockings	68
The Tooth Fairy	69
Fishing	70
Ugly	72
This Week	74

To my parents, Margaret and Gordon,

and my children, Matt and Jess,

with love and thanks

Voices

In the days when children
were seen and not heard
my words were mute
my voice, empty
unable to bypass the invisible
(and arbitrary) line
that accompanied a clip around the ear
or a shotgun glare.

My fingers have learnt
to speak for me.

My own children's self-esteem
appears bulletproof
their words sure-fire.
They open their mouths
and hurl their voices out
into the world.
It seems there is no line
invisible or otherwise.

No one will shoot them down
with ease, least of all me.

Making Tea

When I drink scented tea
infused with citrus
it reminds me
of the time my grandmother
complained to my grandfather
about the pot of tea he had made.
How many times, she asked
as she tossed the contents of the pot
down the drain.
How many times do I have to tell you
to aerate the water
or the brew will be bitter?
Grandad's eyes showed nothing but confusion.
He looked as bewildered and hurt
as a schoolboy
who had tried very hard.
Once he would have reacted
differently
but his memory, wit and personality
had long since faded and stewed
to a murky grey –
the colour of his own
tea making.

Millipedes

The year we separated
there was a plague
of millipedes
and our infestation
was the worst ever
a neighbour said
the colour of our house
attracted them.

Each night I swept
the exterior clean
and by morning
the millipede army was back
tracking its way up
our pale walls
leaving invisible trails
of toxin.

Their invertebrate bodies
like scars or scabs
shaped into spirals
and question marks
and their thousand feathery legs
were tiny sutures
that could not mend
our wounds.

The Shed

Inside the young girl's shed
tadpoles emerge
from frog spawn
and mutate
grow legs, drop tails
morph slowly
into frogpoles or tadlets
she's not sure which
but she tends them
with the meticulous care
and attention
of any good mother –
feeding them
cleaning up after them
changing their environment
regularly
so boredom does not set in.

She catches their food
flies, crickets, moths
even small spiders
tosses the unsuspecting
into the frog den.
She relishes the way they leap
to catch their prey
and enjoys watching them swallow
bugs as big as themselves.

She loves their amphibian beauty –
their slender limbs
the discs on their fingers and toes
the whirring ree-ree-ree
of their night-time song
the way the sun brightens
their golden eyelids
and how their mouths turn up
into a smile.

the hole

the handle broke
split
right down to the bottom
but it's okay
he can do some words
'a' and 'o' and 'n'
comprehension is out of this world
I was calling his name
and he was at the gate
with the hand on the hip
you know, the four year old boss
funny as
I took him to the doctor
and he put him on medication
it is helping
I wondered how long it would take
a couple of weeks maybe
he won't let you forget that pill
he doesn't call it a tablet
he calls it his triangle
the behaviour has picked up
he doesn't get as aggressive
I need those speech assessments
I rang them again yesterday
but it's okay
we're moving forward
he'll play in the dirt
with his truck for ages
he loves the tractor
that's the ants pants

he runs around the backyard
digging up holes
he dug in the sandpit
a hole so deep
he dug right through the plastic
Jeez, a hole that deep
I'm going to have to fill it in

Slowly

(In memory of seven-year-old Shellay Ward)

She stares at stains
the colour of milky tea
on the ceiling
wills them to turn liquid
to rain into her mouth
to nourish her parched tongue
dry as a leather strap.

She dreams of gleaming kitchens
of opening a gently humming fridge
to find white light treasures
of milk and cheese and butter
but the kitchen is another world.
She is confined to the darkness
of her bedroom where
the door remains locked with
a hangman's knot of rope.

Her feather-weight frame
is anchored, too weak
to move beyond the limits
of her rotting mattress
sprawled across the littered floor.
And though she longs for caresses
and sunshine
she lies instead with faeces and urine.

Her smile was once sunny
and her flaming hair, luminous.
It still floats around her like a sun
but her eyes do not shine
instead they sink slowly away
like a sunset.

poetry workshop

behind razor wire and
locked doors
we sit with the girls
and do poetry
attempt to guide them
to express themselves

one has already done so
skilfully
in large capital letters
she's engraved the word
DIE
deep into her arm

someone else writes
a poem
about how much she hates
poetry
about how much she hates
our workshop

I thought they would all
write like that
in a bold screaming font
but some
write with a longing so old
it is almost invisible

about family
about absent fathers
about dying grandmothers

frustration blows in and out
of the room
like a hot breath
papers are torn up
scribbled on
whined about –

you can't taste anger!
one seethes
but even I can taste
the bitterness
on her tongue.

Empty Rooms

She walks from empty room
to empty room
straightening neat beds
opening blinds and sash windows
to give the rooms some light
some life.

The ticking of the kitchen clock
and humming fridge
accompany her
whispering
unwanted premonitions
into the stillness.

She searches for clothes to wash
books to tidy, dust to wipe
knowing it would always
come to this
but knowing
is no consolation.

She thinks of the children
with their father
for the long school holidays
and knows that these empty rooms
will one day too soon
become her future.

In the bathroom

There are remnants
of hair dye, bottled tan and shaving foam
smeared across the front of the bath
the back of the door
the hand towel
and beige floor tiles.
There are bath bombs and crystals
candles and sponges
toothpaste and Listerine
kisses on the mirror.

This bathroom has seen
the battle of adolescence
more than once.

Long gone are the bags of floating toys
rubber ducks and water pistols
the strawberry bubble bath
and the waterbabes
floating on their backs
with suntanned baby chests
rising like brown hills
through white foam
that formed sweet haloes
around impish faces.

Blood Work

As kids we bounced along
the Main North Road
through Gepps Cross
in the back of the old ute
our wind-whipped hair
sheltered by the cab
our noses pinched
and our voices squealing
at the stench of abattoir death.
Back then, a steak sandwich
or a barbecued chop
was not an animal.

Now, all that land has been scraped
blood and guts
scoured from the earth
but the soil still breathes memories
of mutilation
in a place where the stages of grief
death and dying
had no meaning to most

like the meat worker
who told of the young slaughterman
who showed her how
to shoot a bolt through the skull
of a terrified cow
and how they drank and laughed
at her party trick later
at the Meatman's pub.

When I hear the clatter of hooves
in a cattle truck
staggering at the mercy
of each grinding gear shift
I grieve for them
and for the thousands
that leave the killing stalls
and enter the slicing room
to endure amputations
of legs and tails and skin
twitching, writhing: alive.

Tartan

(In memory of Dean Shillingsworth)

Once I would think of woven cloth
of clans called
MacBean, MacBryde and
MacBeth.
I would think of bagpipes
of men wearing kilts
and long socks.

I would think of the Battle of Culloden
of castles and haggis
shortbread and whisky
of glens and bens
and that long-necked monster
hiding in the murky depths
of Loch Ness.

Now I will think of children
fishing for a suitcase
a tartan coffin
with a two-year-old boy
encased in plastic
floating in a pond
with duck weed.

Lilies

While I build poems
and stories in my study
my son builds
a cubby house in the orchard
and my daughter digs
in an untidy garden bed.
Through the window
I notice
small breasts budding
beneath her shirt
like flowers.

Life blooms
even in an absence of focus
like the clusters of lilies
white trumpets on
slender stems
that sprout every year
in the marshy creek bed
even in the garden
where despite the dry winter
and lack of care
they flourish.

Superstition

The number thirteen is
out of bounds
and Friday the 13th
a day to stay at home.
It began when she was a girl with
don't stand on the cracks
or you'll break your back
and grew to other things
like not putting new shoes
on the kitchen table
or opening umbrellas inside
and never walking under ladders.
She avoided black cats
and threw salt over her shoulder
even when she had not spilt it
(just in case).

Now, she cannot serve gravy
unless she has stirred it
sixty times.
The place mats and cutlery
have to sit squarely
or they upset her sense of harmony
her sense of stability.
The sheets have tight hospital corners
the towels are folded lengthwise
and hang with fastidious precision.

Everything exists in an ordered way
even the poker machines
though they appear chaotic
she believes there are patterns
in their randomness
patterns she can tame.

Sex Scene

I decide not to include
the sex scene in the manuscript
worried that someone
might recognise themselves
worried too that someone
might not.

I decide it would be
far too revealing –
I might come across as
overtly sexy
or worse, overtly unsexy.
It might show me up
as a selfish, clumsy or
superficial lover.

Besides, writing about sex
is far too messy
with words dripping on the page
active verbs sliding and
colliding with concrete nouns
like saliva mixing with
other fluids.

I've read some sticky manuscripts
and I don't even want to think
about my parents
or worse, my children
reading anything remotely
sexy or sensual
that I have written.

So there will be no
unzipping of anything
at the door
no rock-hard nipples
crotchless or lacy lingerie
no sucking, licking or slurping
and certainly no sex
of any type
in the car park.

Mrs Brown

We like to have a few
me and my friend June
she comes over with her husband
she's not young, like me she's sixty-three
and we might have a bottle of Brown Brothers
just one
and then we'll get carried away
and we'll say –
Where's Mrs Brown
Go and get us a Mrs Brown from the fridge –
and we'll send the men out
while we talk and talk
and they roll their eyes
cos we might start laughing or crying
and the tears
oh God the tears
we cry and cry
but we're happy
and we'll drink every drop of Mrs Brown
that's in the house
and then June and her husband'll stay the night
you know cos they've drunk too much
to drive home
and the next day
oh God it's terrible
we feel awful – really, really sick
but we love a drink we do
we love our Mrs Brown.

Alien

He lies like a corpse
in bed till three in the afternoon
six feet tall
oozing testosterone
intent on one goal –
his social calendar.

His room is a battleground
of half drunk coffee cups
plates with decomposing food
half-read books and
discarded clothes –
mostly his.

We talk of the future
he listens with his ears
turned toward the television
and a dead man's glaze
that tells me he is blind
to my ranting.

He has his own agenda
will do his own thing
in his own good time.
I try not to panic
in the presence of this alien
whose strange ways

and odd smell
have invaded the house.
I can only hope
an embryo of wisdom
planted before puberty will
take hold and eventually grow.

At Twelve

One minute she is galloping
her grown-up body
through long-grassed paddocks
neighing like a horse and laughing
as the dog snaps her heals
or squatting next to the muddy dam
whilst fishing for tadpoles and frog spawn
or digging up worms.

The next minute she is clip-clopping
in high-heeled shoes
straightening her long mane of hair
and thinking about colour
or washing a mud-mask from her face
digging dirt from her fingernails
then polishing and filing them
into an adult shape.

Thirteen

She rolls mascara eyes
at our old jokes
and sleeps till noon.
The quilt cover
with the pony pattern
and cuddly toys
get packed away.
She'd rather have nothing
on the quilt
nothing to remind her
she was a child.

She kisses her frogs
goodbye
sells them to the pet shop.
The rabbit and guinea pig
are left to roam free
in the garden
content
like the cat and dog
not to be dressed
in dolls clothes
any more.

She has traded them all
for an eternity
of conversations
on the mobile phone
and computer –
MSN and MySpace.
She hangs
with boys instead
hoping perhaps
that they will turn
into princes.

Sewing (the artist's wife)

(1913 oil painting by Hans Heysen)

At the window
infused in a creamy glow
she leans
in concentration.

Each stroke of his brush
captures light
and love.

And at the nape
of her sensuous neck
where her hair is wound
into a gentle scroll

it is as if each stroke
of his brush
is a kiss.

Gone!

Sixteen years of dinners,
of school lunches,
of early breakfasts and
tri-weekly washing.

Sixteen years of reminders to
clean-up your room
do your homework and
eat your dinner – please!

Sixteen years of refereeing
of praising, guiding, arguing and
Jeez! I can't bloody wait
to have a minute's peace!

Sixteen years and they've gone
left me to my own quiet house
left me in peace – finally
to do as I please

to become the person I was
or the person I want to be
while they holiday overseas
for three weeks!

After sixteen years I am suspended
between silence and possibility
and in the impossible stillness
of dinner for one and a tidy house

I do nothing and become no one.

Teenage Retreat

He is like smoke
I cannot grasp
cannot see through –

a thick fog of torment.

I can smell his presence
but he is untouchable
often unfathomable –

a lazy, hazy mystery.

Occasionally he materialises
and we might fight a fire
together

but then he will vanish

burn and smoulder
or spontaneously combust
and once again become a cloud

of uncertainty.

Insomnia

Last night my mind chased away dreams
zeroed-in on unimportant details
worried about nothing in particular
and fidgeted with anything
and everything
like a child
with a hyperactive disorder.

In sleep deprived desperation
I reminded myself
of research that suggests
ADHD is often misdiagnosed
is sometimes the result
of bad parenting
so I resolved to be firm –

I told my restless spirit
to behave, to settle down
or else!
But it refused to stay still
to sit in one spot
and let calmness descend.

Instead it sprinted, darted
and dodged
every sheep counting
deep-breathing, sleep-inducing tactic

until finally
in the luminous dawn
it fled, exhausted
and left me at last to drift off
with the warbling magpies
and rumbling trucks.

I had one glorious, unconscious hour
before I had to peel myself
out of my cursed bed
and get on with my day –
dazed as an over-medicated child.

Still Living

The flowers in our crystal vase
have long ago died
apart from a few chrysanthemums
still bright yellow
and sparky as cheerleader pompoms.

The others
the carnations, dahlias and roses
wither and droop
like sad women crying.

They sit in rancid water
that stains the glass
their floral perfume replaced
with the pungent scent
of decay

and yet I'm reluctant
to throw out the bouquet
when something is
still clinging to life.

A Starlit Sky

You rattled the locked box
I carried
full of paper-thin hopes and promises.

Beneath the branches of the ghost gum
you held up questions
against a starlit sky.

Why? you asked
and I answered. I always had answers
tangled with lies.

That night the moon cut a circle
in the darkness
and when we held hands and kissed

folded in your warm breath
was a slip
of tongue that held the truth.

Washday Pockets

A rubber band
Two silver screws
A rusty cigarette lighter
One green marble
Plastic wrap with cake crumbs
from recess

A love heart stamp
A five-cent piece
Watermelon lip gloss
Two fluoro hair ties
One long thick horse hair

Two business cards
One ballpoint pen
A slip of paper
A phone number
A woman's name

Walking

For one year we walked
twice a week
for three kilometres
we worked things through
discussed ideas and feelings
reflected and bounced them
off the pavement.

In the cold nights
our thoughts became
thick and heavy
with condensation.
In the summer a shimmer of sweat
accompanied our fears
and desires

and in that time
you pounded away
at the grief
that gripped your heart
while I carved out
a new path
walked towards a new life.

Ironing Sheets

Outside, the cerulean sea
and sky are knitted together
by the hazy Peloponnese horizon.
White houses line steep cliffs
and stone steps echo
the bray and slow clip clop
of donkeys.

Inside, there isn't even a fan
to stir the dreamy heat infused air.
The iron spits and steams
the pensione sheets stiff
as the sails of yachts
and white
as the Greek boy's smile.

Burnt

I take the silver in front of me
the knife and fork
and begin to carve the space
between us.
That heavy, laden weighty space
that sits like overcooked steak.

I slice and cut and carve
with difficulty as you watch
silenced by my persistence perhaps
or by what I have uncovered.
Maybe you are startled
by what I have revealed –

nothing worth consuming,
nothing left to work with.
Clearly, we can't even grind it
into mince
or reinvent it as another dish
with some spice or sauce
to dress it up.

As a final gesture
when I have placed my silver down
you spear a portion
of charred remains
and lift it for inspection
where it hovers briefly
along with your silent acceptance.

Suburban Villanelle

She makes the most of every day
Changes nappies without a frown
What more is there to do or say?

She unpegs clothes, puts them away
Dressed in her old blue dressing gown
She makes the most of every day

She cleans the dirty litter tray
For the cat he said he'd like to drown
What more is there to do or say?

She opens the fridge, finds decay
Lettuce leaves wilting, turning brown
She makes the most of every day

The children shout and fight, role-play
She yells for them to 'turn it down!'
What more is there to do or say?

Her husband phones late, says he may
work on, have dinner, stay in town
She makes the most of every day
What more is there to do or say?

Weeds

It's the weekly drop-off
and for the first time in a year
I pull up outside his house
in the daylight
to deliver our daughter.

I sit in the car and contemplate
his lacklustre garden – tall with weeds
the discarded, greying newspapers
sprawling pile of firewood
and letter box spewing junk mail.

Suddenly a sense of guilt erupts
for not having the courage
to leave in the early days
when it might have been easier
but now he is older –

perhaps too old
to cultivate a new life
and I feel sorry
for the bad years wasted
and the good years gone.

I drive home in the fading light
with sad songs drifting from the radio.
When I pull into my own drive
and look closely at my garden
for the first time, I see weeds.

Let's Play

Every week we go
together.
We have a meal in the pub
and get a cupful of coins
a cupful of fun
and promise.
You never know your luck!
And we play –
him on his machine
me on mine.
We swap glances
and look over shoulders
at free spins and bonuses.
We watch the tally rise and rise
and fall
and fall.
We have our wins and
now'n'again
we take home a pocketful of loot.

On the days that I go
alone
no one bothers me.
A woman is as invisible
as a pokie player's joy.
I don't tell him –
he doesn't need to know.
It's best to have a little mystery
in a relationship
don't you think?

Besides what else am I supposed to do
now the kids have grown up?
How do you fill a long day
tidying up a clean house?
The day-time drama on the telly
doesn't cut it any more.
Here is where the drama is
here with golden dreams
watching the world spin
and turn
spin and turn.

She-Mail

His heart beats like the cursor
flashing on the blank screen.

He would like to greet her
in person with a smile

but the thudding in his heart
and the knotting in his throat

overwhelm
and he becomes void of words

empty of promises
his mind vacant as the screen.

Instead, he sits watching
the cursor blinking

marking time, hinting
at their potential

and waits for her
to fill his inbox

with love.

Without Punctuation Marks

I am writing
an interrupted solo

my daughter comes to show me
how she can pop the buttons on her jeans
when she stretches her belly
seven times

I smile and nod
impressed
and turn back to my writing

till my son leaps through the door
stretches himself out
on the floor
and does ten grunting push-ups

I have to be fit he explains
rises and walks out

don't shut the door I say
leave it open

I turn back to my desk
and wonder if this is why
I like to write
without punctuation marks

Insomniac dreams

You want me to get up
won't let me sleep
I'm exhausted
have been haunted
by insomnia for days on end
and yet you disturb me
pull me from my sleepy bed
by my arms
and make me stand before you
like a rag doll.

And you can't see why I am angry
why I am so tired
you think I am being unreasonable
when I start throwing pillows
and my voice around the room.
You think I am being ridiculous
when I pound the wall with my fists
and cry about how tired I am
and how hard it will be for me
to get back to sleep.

You do not understand how
when I wake some time later
with the remnants of the dream
clinging to me like the smell
of damp hair on a pillow
why when I roll over
and find your peaceful face
looking so rested
you cannot understand
why I am so annoyed at you.

Driving Lessons

The first times out were difficult
with me trying to synchronise
the clutch and accelerator
and brake at the right time
kangaroo hopping and crunching
through the gears
whilst trying to negotiate
the traffic.

Dad and I left our
parent/teen relationship at home
and firmly buckled up
our impatient natures.
He talked calmly and I did my best
to listen
to hour upon hour of instructions:

Watch out for the parked car
Keep an eye on the road ahead
Remember your blind spot
Be prepared for anything
You never know what's coming
from behind.

After many hours we managed
to negotiate our differences
smoothly
except when I failed a hill start
and went rolling backward.

Dad seized the handbrake
while I rode the clutch
and accelerated.
Clouds of smoke pumped out
of Dad's ears
as the wheels spun and
we hurtled through a red light.

A professional driving instructor
was hired to prepare me
for the final test.
He was my father's age
his instructions were similar
but I didn't like his hands-on approach
nor the fact that he taught me
how to negotiate
more than just the traffic.

Mother & Child

(For Maud and Lilli)

At forty, you, the sibling babysitter
the paediatric nurse, the nanny
the lactation consultant
the always caring
for other people's children
still have none of your own

and then the miracle
IVF
finally pays off
and your own precious child is born
and together, the two of you
are family.

The Old Lifts

The old lifts take an age to arrive
providing the time to stare ahead
and gather your breath
before you tackle the trolley drive
up and down the choice-heavy
aisles of Coles.

A crowd gathers as you wait
and you ready yourself
for the inevitable conversation –
Bloody lifts
Have to be the slowest in Adelaide
Slower than a wet week
And unreliable
Don't know how many people
have been trapped inside.

Finally, an unsteady grinding announces
the arrival of one lift
and you wait
for the sluggish doors to part
before you enter, press the 'down' button
and wait for the sluggish doors to close.

You grin at the person shaking his head
at the sleepy ride down
and the conversation starts again
Are we even moving?
Ah here we go
Slowest bloody lifts in Adelaide
We've been stuck in here before
Who hasn't?

The light flickers and the lift shudders
as it lands on the ground floor
and when the sluggish doors finally open
you all breathe a sigh of relief
that you have managed to escape
another claustrophobic lift trapping.

Later, there is news
posters announce
the installation of new lifts
soon!

It takes six months to install one lift
so the slow rides continue
slower than ever
with only one lift to rely on
it struggles with the added burden
seems to shudder more
take even longer
providing plenty of time and reason
to grumble and joke with fellow passengers
or meditate
if you happened to be on your own.

Eventually the new lift is operational
You walk up, press the button
the lift arrives, you step inside
It is clean, shiny, metallic.
People shuffle in
you all nod and murmur your approval.

You press the down button
Listen briefly to the drone of the exhaust fan
within a second you have landed
and a voice announces your arrival
Ground floor.

The gleaming doors slip apart
and as you step away you hear
an old voice say
*No time for meditation
or conversation now*
and you realise the doors have closed
on a little piece of history
a little piece of community.

Bricks

Years ago they were a family
of six – two adults and four children
who peeled and mashed potatoes
shelled peas and stirred gravy
for the Sunday roast.

Now, her life has compressed
to a frozen block
complete with a list
of sodium, trans-fatty acids
artificial colours and flavouring.

Meals have reduced to small bricks
of flavoured ice
dressed in plastic and cardboard
to place in the microwave
to heat and eat

Alone.

Father and Son

Each day I drive home
from work
with the tired day
trailing behind me

impatient with the traffic
cursing at thoughtless drivers
rushing to catch
the lights

until I see the father
with his Down's Syndrome child
who is now a man –
the two men

walk slowly
hand in hand
placing one patient step
after another.

Winter

Her hair is string
and the way she stands is
marionette tense

as if an invisible puppeteer
looms overhead

pulling her into a contorted
or tortured pose.

Her skin is chalk
pale as the ash
she rakes in the grate.

She pokes the fire with a broken stick
of herself
watches it char the edges

as she turns over flaming wood
embers leap
glitter then disappear

like sparks of memory
or the antiquated desires
of her youth

that glisten
like silken cobwebs in the corners
of her mind.

Breath

She perches on the edge
of her bed
on the edge of life
a broken bird
humpbacked
with porous bones
and grim vertical-lined lips.

The tubes in her nose
pass oxygen to her lungs
incapable of filling themselves
after a life-time of too many fags
too many children and
too many years of poverty
with a drunken husband
who left her with six kids.

She soldiered on alone
accessing the food agencies
when necessary
kept breathing in and out
drawing deeply
on those tobacco sticks
filling her lungs with smoke
her elixir

but the bitterness bled
into her bones
turned them to ash
and now in the nursing home
there is no breath
there is no relief
just tubes
and the hiss and hum
of the oxygen.

Cooking

In the kitchen
she stared into pans
and stirred gravy absently
in a mist of steam
amid simmering pots
and the smell
of roasting meat

or stared endlessly
out of the kitchen window
beyond the green garden
her hands wrinkling
in steaming water
a cigarette smouldering
in a nearby ashtray
and a long curl of smoke
spiralling upwards
in the sedate air

while I balanced stork-like
or hopped from foot to foot
and talked to her
angular profile
told her about my day
and watched
my excited chatter
extinguish
in the cloudy space
between us.

Years later
in my own home
I found that hazy space
my own hands wrinkling
in cooling dishwater
and my eyes averted
to a less domestic setting.

Beneath a blue moon

We sit on your old couch
stare up at the full moon
looming in the night sky
and argue
what is means to be blue.

I say it is when two moons
occur in the same month
or when the moon is the colour blue
caused by dust particles
or volcanic ash.

You say it is Old English
a 'belewe' moon was an extra moon
occurring before Lent
the word could mean either 'blue'
or 'betrayer'.

We hold hands and grin at the irony
of three betrayers glowing in the dark
and agree whatever it means
it is something special
something rare.

With Green Stockings

(1939 watercolour by Paul Klee)

She is a dozen lines
connected and unconnected
looking up
to the sun in the sky.

She is a geometric puzzle
her square eyes
divided by her nose
are numerator and denominator
her mouth is a single digit
and her ears are two question marks.

She is splotches of colour –
her hair is a wash of orange rust
her dress is blue spotted
her stockings, green
and her upturned arms
are sunshine yellow.

She is a drawing
holding the universe
in her arms.

The Tooth Fairy

She's like a fairy godmother
with her short grey bob
her tiny look-over-the-top glasses
and sugar-frosted smile.

She kindly touches my arm
listens intently to all my news
sympathises over my recent virus
and asks about the children.

Even though I know she can't be
more than a few years older than me
I am drawn into her fairy godmotherly fold
and relax into the deep cushiony chair

But brace myself when she positions her mask
and picks up her wand, that tool
that feels harder and harsher
than in any other hands.

She grinds away in sensitive spots
gouges at stains that won't budge
and offers a gentle 'so sorry' when I flinch
repeatedly in the chair.

At home, there is pain
I run my tongue along bleeding, swollen gums
I read the return visit card in my hand
and wonder why I choose to see her again.

Fishing

She dangled her line, her photo
into a sea of internet daters
alongside all the other hopeful anglers.

Instantly she had a few bites
who unfortunately turned out to be nothing
but tiddlers and ugly old gropers

Then finally she reeled in
something she was pleased with –
a real catch

though in the end it was clear
he too was a no hoper
one that changed colour with the tide

to disguise the truth.
A puffer fish who inflated himself
pretended to be bigger than he was.

Now it was painfully obvious
that he didn't ever belong to that school
or have the car, the job, the house

he boasted of
didn't have any of the riches
just his bloated self.

But she fell for it
hook, line and sinker
until he sunk himself with one too many

inflated boastings
and under scrutiny his story became
more and more fishy

so she dredged the murky bottom
until each one of his scaly lies
surfaced

and she began to see him
as the slippery eel and scum-sucking catfish
he really was.

She tossed him back
into the dark internet waters
and moved on.

Realising that fishing is a patient sport
she re-baited her hook, changed the sinker
and cast out once again.

Ugly

How would you feel to be labelled fat
just because your metabolism
is slow, unsteady, perhaps unstable?
How would you like to be called ugly
just because you have a few hairs
on your chinny-chin-chin?

And how is it fair that someone
can be labelled beautiful, stunning even
just because they are born slender
with smooth skin, tiny hands and feet
and toe nails as pretty as jewels?

I believe we can all scrub up well.
Remember that old saying –
There are no ugly women
just lazy ones?
Well, I subscribe to that philosophy.

If you give a duster or scrubbing brush
to any fair maiden and get her to clean
the toilet bowl or the fireplace
eventually she too will resemble
that coal-dusty rag in her chafed hands.

And conversely if you put me in a coach
shaped like the proverbial pumpkin
with matching gown and glass slippers
would I not look the part of princess?
Well, I ask you, sister, who wouldn't?
But then to run away
to play hard to get with a charming man
a prince no less!
Well, that takes more than beauty
that takes arrogance.
And let's face it, arrogance is not attractive.

And finally to add insult
to my already injured pride
my feet are sized up
by a slipper that could only fit a child.
I ask you, what sort of man chases feet
the size of a prepubescent adolescent?

This Week

At work this week a man with a spider web
tattoo on his face and a Parkinson's shake
in one hand told me that last week he had left
a one hundred-dollar bill on the counter
and in a past life he had donated thousands
to our office and that is why we should give him
a food voucher. Now!

At work this week a man holding a creased
plastic bag, wearing bright green track pants said
Daylight Saving is a terrible thing and politicians
don't care. They're lazy bitches who should try
and live on the Disability Support Pension
and feed a family.

At work this week I visited a nursing home
smiled at unseeing people in wheelchairs
breathed in the scent of ageing, spent thirty minutes
chatting to a woman about her finances and lifted
the flat-line of her day.

At work this week a man who looked like a young
Simon Townsend leaned on the counter, smiled
as widely as a celebrity, pulled a soft purple toy
from his pocket and asked to be photographed with it.

At work this week a one-legged woman drowsy
from prescription medication demanded we pay
her car registration despite the fact that she could
only walk a crooked line to the front door
and did not manage to slam it as she left.

At work this week a man with a shaved head
a long goatee beard and a smack-you-in-the-face voice
forgot the name written on his ID. Wrote David
instead of Damien and signed with Victor.

At work this week we learnt that a long-term client
with an intellectual disability was found dead
after six weeks. His mother said she needed
help to remove his mattress. It was stained with
his blood.

At work this week a young woman with no teeth
a black mop of hair and thick wobbly thighs yelled
'Go the Power', called me 'Shazza, ya old bag'
and told me to get a real job.

www.ingramcontent.com/pod-product-compliance
Lightning Source LLC
Chambersburg PA
CBHW062152100526
44589CB00014B/1801